Guitar PRIMER

by Mel Bay

Audio Contents

Online Audio

www.melbay.com/93197MEB

T0001541

MEL BAY ®

WWW.MELBAY.COM

The purpose of the **Mel Bay Primer for Guitar** is to:

Supply the teacher with adequate
teaching material for early beginners,
regardless of age.

Bring the instrument to very young pupils,
widening the scope of student selectivity.

Help the teacher promote a better
understanding of music theory and its
application to the guitar.

Make learning the guitar
a joyful activity.

Table of Contents

The Rudiments of Music

The Staff

Music is written on a **staff** consisting of **five lines** and **four spaces**.

The lines and spaces are numbered upward as shown:

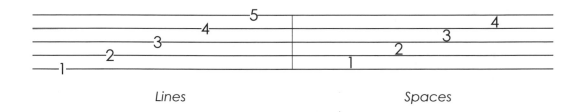

Lines   Spaces

They also have **letter** names.

The **lines** are named as follows: 1 – E, 2 – G, 3 – B, 4 – D, 5 – F.

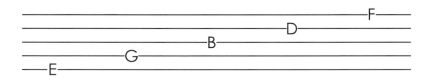

The letters can easily be remembered by the sentence *Every Good Boy Does Fine*.

The letter names of the **spaces** are: 1 – F, 2 – A, 3 – C, 4 – E.

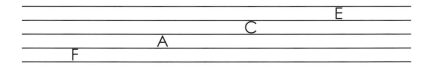

They spell the word *F – A – C – E*.

The musical alphabet has seven letters — A, B, C, D, E, F, G.

The Clef

This sign  is the **treble** or **G clef**.

All guitar music is written in this clef.

The **staff** is divided into **measures** by vertical lines called **bars**.

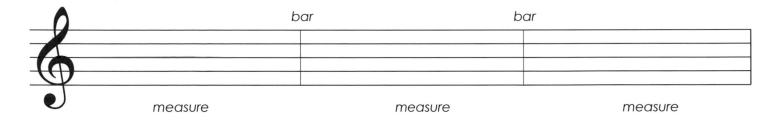

Double bars mark the end of a section or strain of music.

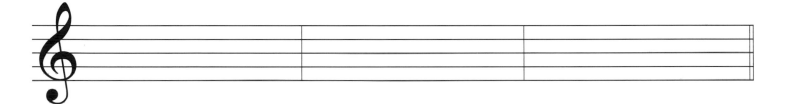

Review

1. Please fill in the missing words in the following sentences.

2. Music is written on a _____ consisting of _____ *lines* and _____ *spaces*.

3. The *lines* and *spaces* are numbered _____.

4. They also have _____ names.

5. The *lines* are named as follows: _____, _____, _____, _____, _____.

6. The *spaces* are named _____, _____, _____, _____.

7. The musical alphabet has _____ letters; they are _____, _____, _____, _____, _____, _____, _____, _____.

8. All guitar music is written in the _____ clef.

9. The **staff** is divided into _____ by vertical lines called _____.

Notes

This is a note.

A note can have three parts:

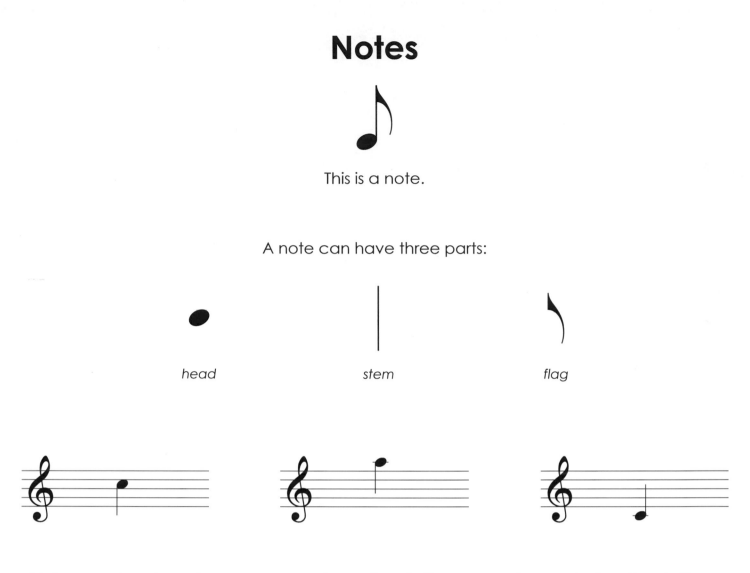

head   stem   flag

Notes may be placed within the staff,   above the staff,   and   below the staff.

A note will bear the name of the line or space it occupies on the staff.

The location of a note in, above or below the staff will indicate the **pitch**.

PITCH

The highness or lowness of a tone.

TONE

A musical sound.

The **shape** of a note will indicate the **length** of its sound.

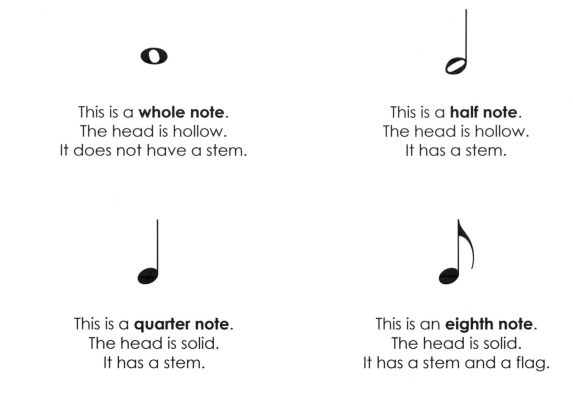

This is a **whole note**.
The head is hollow.
It does not have a stem.

This is a **half note**.
The head is hollow.
It has a stem.

This is a **quarter note**.
The head is solid.
It has a stem.

This is an **eighth note**.
The head is solid.
It has a stem and a flag.

Rests

A **rest** is a sign used to designate a period of silence. This period of silence will be of the same duration of time as the note to which it corresponds.

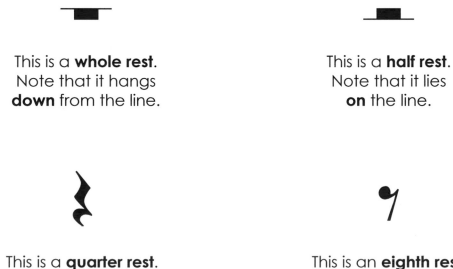

This is a **whole rest**.
Note that it hangs
down from the line.

This is a **half rest**.
Note that it lies
on the line.

This is a **quarter rest**.

This is an **eighth rest**.

Notes and Comparative Rests

NOTES	𝅝	𝅗𝅥	♩	♪
	Whole 4 counts	Half 2 counts	Quarter 1 count	Eighth 2 for 1 count
RESTS	▬	▬	𝄽	𝄾

Time Signatures

At the beginning of every piece of music there is a time signature. The top figure indicates the number of counts per measure. The bottom figure indicates the type of note that receives one count. If the lower number is a 4, a quarter note (♩) has been chosen to represent one count. We will learn later how figures other than 4 are sometimes used as the lower number.

Three examples of time signatures

A large C thus: **C** signifies so called "common time"
and is simply another way of designating $\frac{4}{4}$ time.

The Rule of the Dot

A dot placed after a note or a rest increases it's time value by one half.

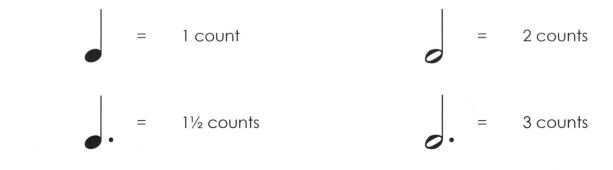

♩ = 1 count   𝅗𝅥 = 2 counts

♩. = 1½ counts   𝅗𝅥. = 3 counts

Note Review

1. A note can have _____ parts.

2. They are the _____, the _____ and the _____.

3. Notes may be placed _____ the staff.

4. Notes may be placed _____ the staff.

5. Notes may be placed _____ the staff.

6. A note will bear the name of the _____ or _____ it occupies.

7. _____ The height or depth of a tone.

8. _____ A musical sound.

9. The _____ of a note will indicate the _____ of its sound.

10. A whole note has a _____.

11. The _____ is hollow.

12. It does not have a _____.

13. A half note has two parts. They are the _____ and _____. The head is _____.

14. A quarter note has two parts. They are the _____ and _____. The head is _____.

15. An eighth note has three parts.

16. They are the _____, the _____ and the _____. The head is _____.

Rest Review

17. A _____ is a sign of _____.

18. This period of _____ will be of the same _____ of _____ as the _____ to which it corresponds.

19. A whole rest hangs _____ from the line.

20. A half rest _____ the line.

21. Draw three quarter rests. _____

22. Draw three eighth rests. _____

The Fingerboard

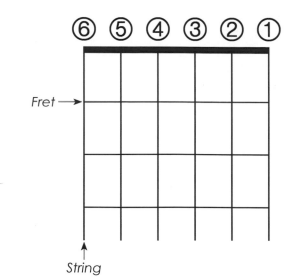

Fret →

String ↑

The vertical lines are the **strings**.
The horizontal lines are the **frets**.
The encircled numbers are the number of the strings.

Reading from left to right the strings will be ⑥ ⑤ ④ ③ ② ①

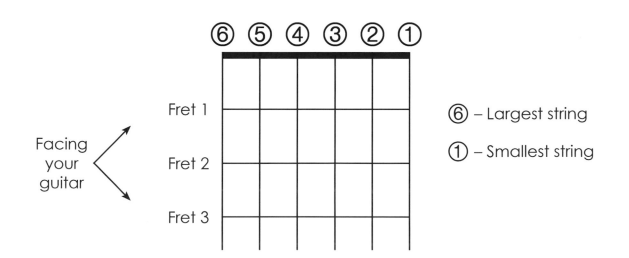

Fret 1

Facing
your
guitar

Fret 2

Fret 3

⑥ – Largest string

① – Smallest string

String numbers: The encircled numbers 6 5 4 3 2 1 will be the numbers of the **strings**.

The Correct Way to Hold the Guitar

This is the Pick

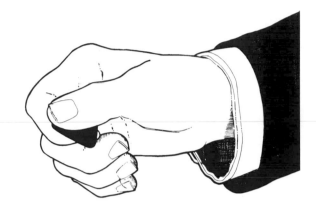

Hold it in this manner firmly between the thumb and first finger.

Down Stroke

Down stroke: This sign () indicates the down-stroke of the pick. The pick should come to rest against the next string to prevent it from being stroked.

Down stroke of the pick.

Striking the Strings

The Left Hand   The Left-Hand Position

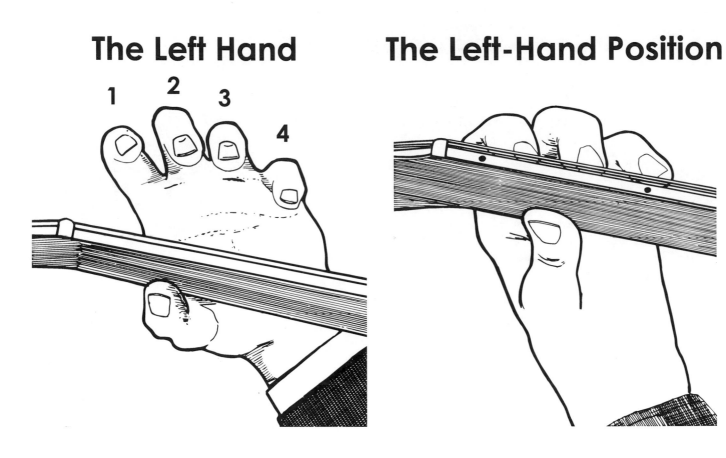

Place your fingers **firmly** on the strings **directly behind the frets**.

Ledger Lines

When the pitch of a musical sound is below or above the staff, the notes are placed on or between extra lines called ledger lines.

They will be like this:

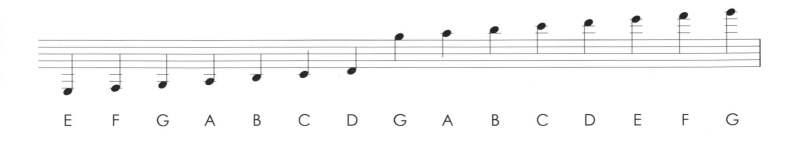

E   F   G   A   B   C   D   G   A   B   C   D   E   F   G

Tuning the Guitar

The six open strings of the guitar will be of the same pitch as the six notes shown in the illustration of the piano keyboard. Note that five of the strings are below the middle C of the piano keyboard.

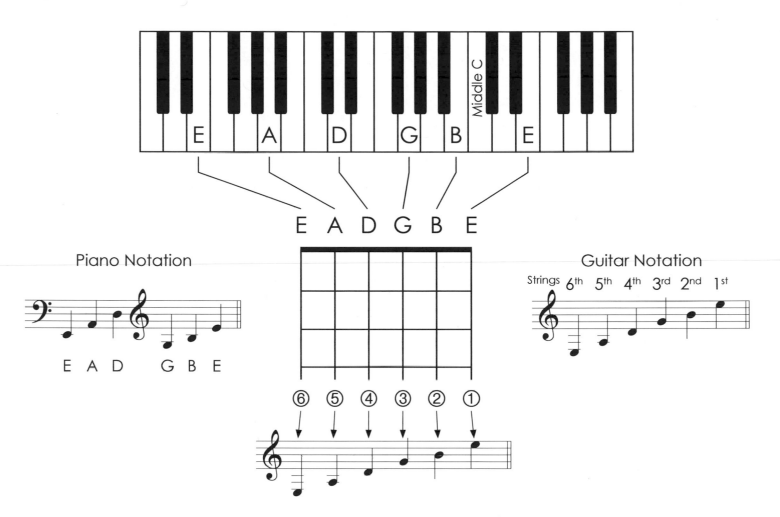

Another Method of Tuning

1. Tune the 6th string in unison to the E or twelfth white key to the left of middle C on the piano.
2. Place a finger behind the fifth fret of the 6th string. This will give you the tone or pitch of the 5th string. (A)
3. Place a finger behind the fifth fret of the 5th string to get the pitch of the 4th string. (D)
4. Repeat the same procedure to obtain the pitch of the 3rd string. (G)
5. Place a finger behind the fourth fret of the 3rd string to get the pitch of the 2nd string. (B)
6. Place a finger behind the fifth fret of the 2nd string to get the pitch of the 1st string. (E)

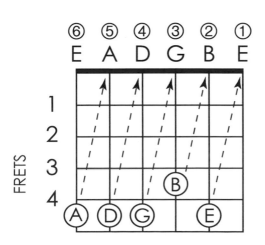

Track 2

Electronic Tuners

Electronic guitar tuners are available at your music store. They are a handy device and highly recommends.

How to practice:

1. Play *slowly* and evenly.
2. Place your fingers *firmly* on the strings *directly behind the frets.*
3. Be *relaxed* at all times.
4. *Count aloud* and *beat your quarter beats with the left foot.*

The Notes on the First String (E)

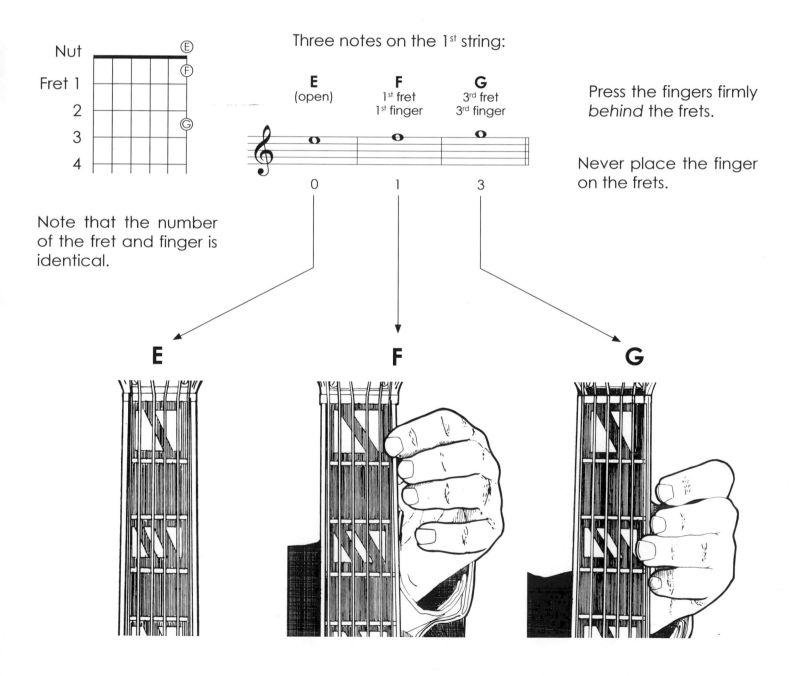

Nut

Fret 1

2

3

4

Three notes on the 1st string:

E	F	G
(open)	1st fret	3rd fret
	1st finger	3rd finger

0   1   3

Press the fingers firmly *behind* the frets.

Never place the finger on the frets.

Note that the number of the fret and finger is identical.

E   F   G

| **o** | A **whole note** receives **four beats**. |

The Fullback

Slow

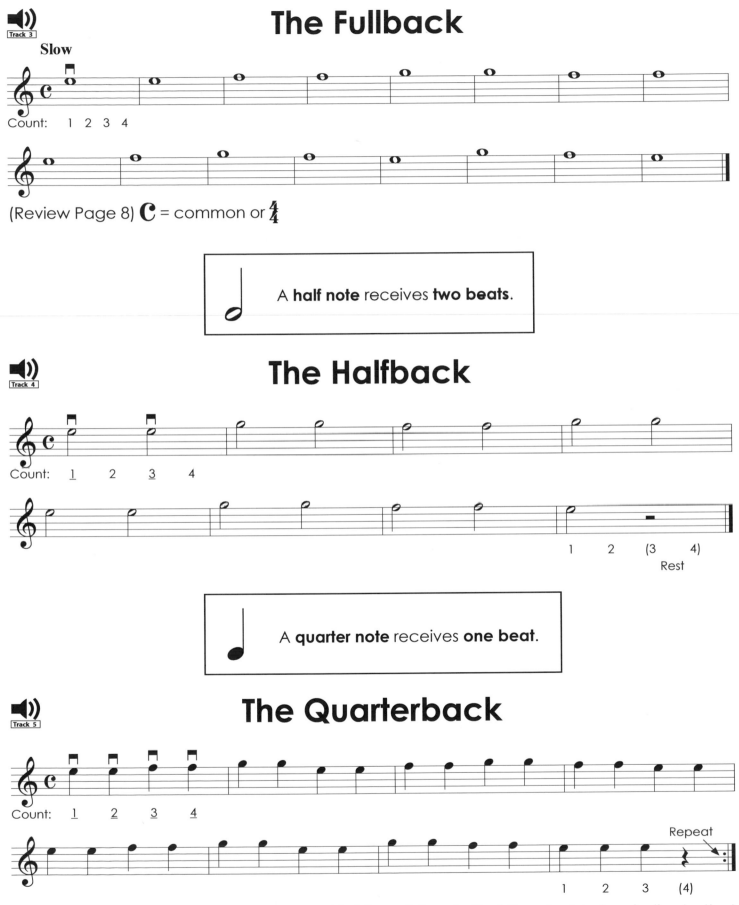

Count: 1 2 3 4

(Review Page 8) **C** = common or **4/4**

| **𝅗𝅥** | A **half note** receives **two beats**. |

The Halfback

Count: 1 2 3 4

1 2 (3 4)
Rest

| **♩** | A **quarter note** receives **one beat**. |

The Quarterback

Count: 1 2 3 4

Repeat

1 2 3 (4)

The dots placed above and below the third line of the staff at the double bar indicate that the piece is to be repeated.

Introducing the "A" Note

A
5th fret *
4th finger

5

Three-Four Time

This sign indicates three-four time.

3 —— beats per measure
4 —— type of note receiving one beat (quarter note)

In three-four time, we will have three beats per measure. A quarter note will receive one beat.

Dotted Half Notes

A dot (•) placed behind a note increases its value by one half. A dotted half note (𝅗𝅥.) will receive three beats.

🔊
Track 6

The First Waltz

* The new "A" note: 1st string, 5th fret, 4th finger.

The Notes on the Second String (B)

Three notes on the 2nd string:

B
(open)

C
1st fret
1st finger

D
3rd fret
3rd finger

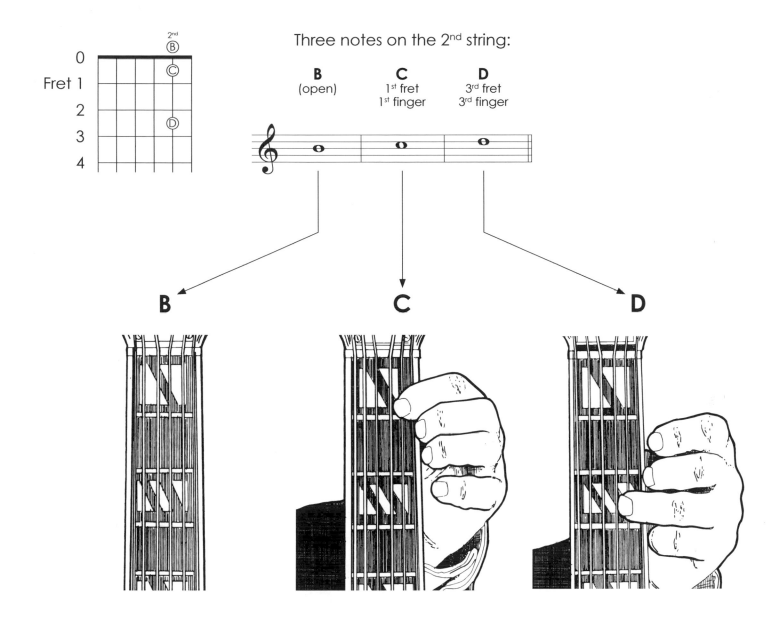

Track 7

Whole Notes

Count: 1 2 3 4

Track 8

Half Notes

Count: 1 2 3 4

Quarter Notes

Count: 1   2   3   4

Topsy-Turvy

The Merry Men

Mexican Waltz

Oh, Suzannah
Study on 1st and 2nd strings

Stephen Foster

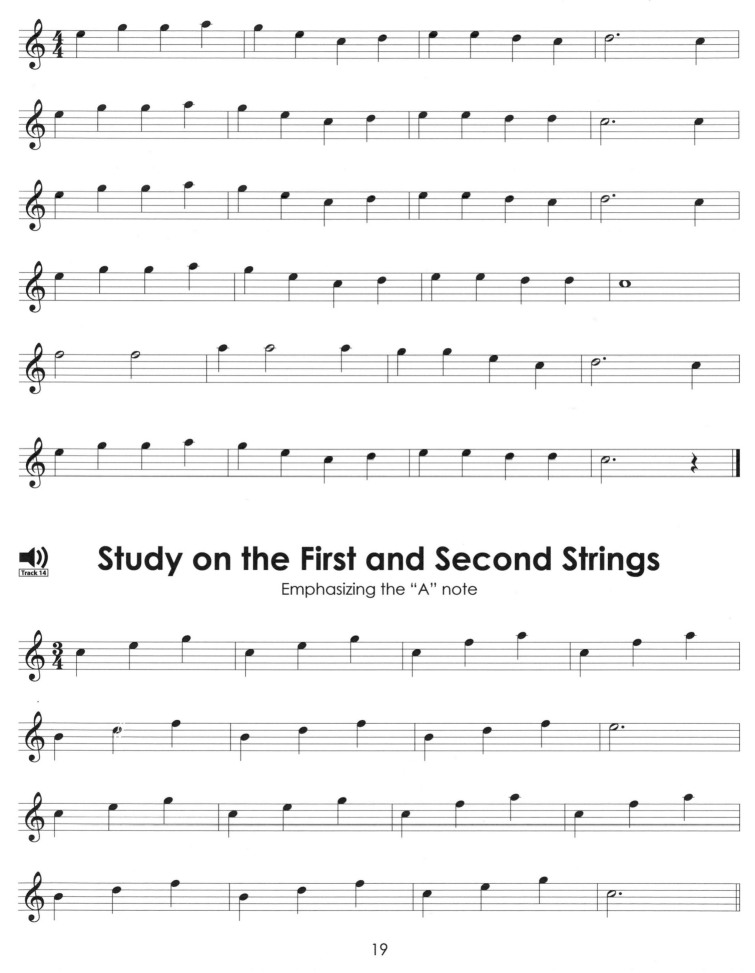

Study on the First and Second Strings
Emphasizing the "A" note

More on the 1st and 2nd strings

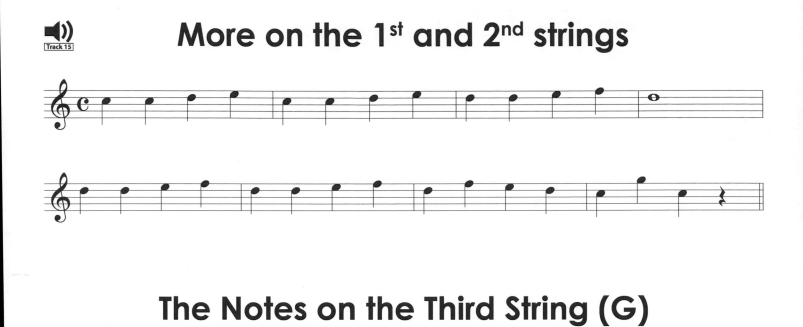

The Notes on the Third String (G)

Two notes on the 3rd string:

G
(open)

A
2nd fret
2nd finger

0   2

G   A

A Study on the Third String

Count: 1 2 3 4

Sparkling Stella

Gee-Bee

This study is played entirely on the 2ⁿᵈ and 3ʳᵈ strings.

Count: 1   2   3   4

Yankee Doodle
Study on the 1st, 2nd and 3rd strings.

Long, Long Ago
Review of 1st three strings

Boat Song

London Bridge

Now that you have learned the notes on the first three strings, look up the song "*Blue Tail Fly*" in the Mel Bay Publication *Fun with the Guitar* and play the melody line.

Goodnight Ladies

The Tie

The **tie** is a curved line between two notes of the same pitch. The first note is played and held for the time duration of both. The second note is not played, but held.

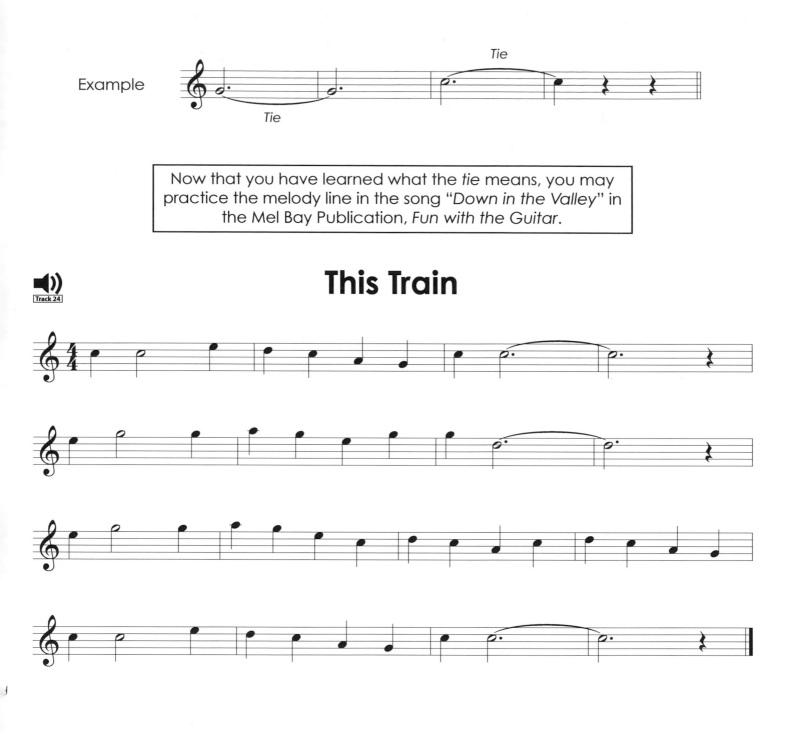

Now that you have learned what the *tie* means, you may practice the melody line in the song "*Down in the Valley*" in the Mel Bay Publication, *Fun with the Guitar*.

This Train

Track 24

Pick-Up Notes

When a song begins with an incomplete measure, the notes in this measure are referred to as **pick-up notes**. When counting time, the last measure, plus the **pick-up notes**, will add up to a complete measure.

Red River Valley

Observe the two pick-up notes in the incomplete measure at the beginning and the two beats in the last measure, thus forming a complete measure.

We Won't Go Home Until Morning

Observe the two pick-up notes in the incomplete measure at the beginning (*) and the two beats in the last measure (**), thus forming a complete measure.

The Notes on the Fourth String (D)

Three notes on the 4th string:

D	**E**	**F**
(open)	1st fret	3rd fret
	1st finger	3rd finger

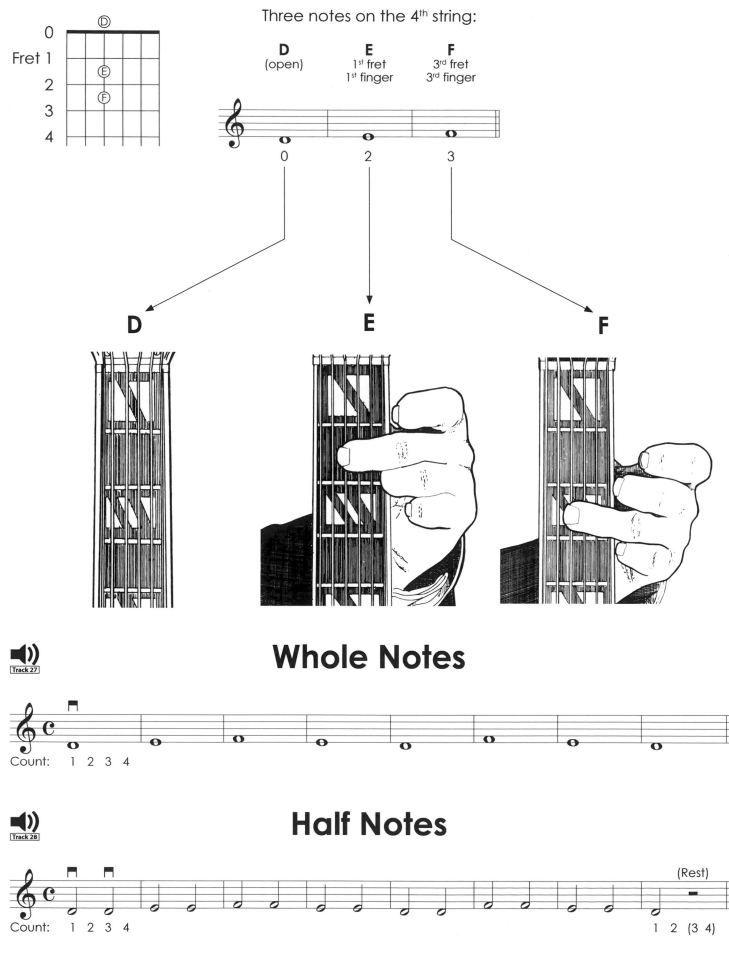

Whole Notes

Count: 1 2 3 4

Half Notes

Count: 1 2 3 4
       (Rest)
       1 2 (3 4)

Quarter Notes

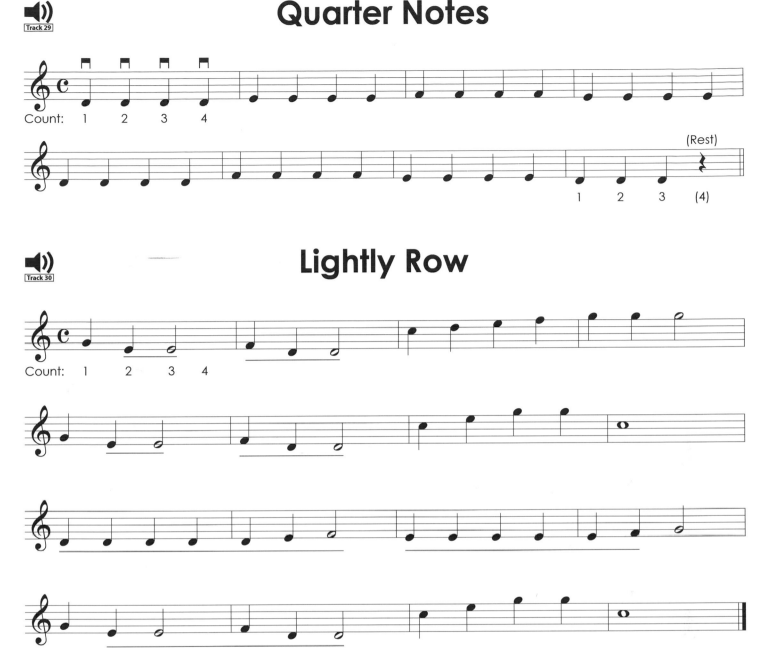

Count: 1   2   3   4

(Rest)

1   2   3   (4)

Lightly Row

Count: 1   2   3   4

All of the underlined notes in the above song are the new notes you are learning on the D or 4th string.

The Bucking Bronco

(*) With the exception of the two underlined notes, *Bucking Bronco* is simply a review of the 1st three strings.

Old McDonald's Farm

Repeat Review

Dots after and before a double bar mean repeat the measures between them.

The Repeater

(*) Notice that the repeat signs include only the last eight measures.

When the Saints Go Marching In Boogie

(*) Observe pick-up notes.   (**) Note that the last measure is incomplete.

Count: 2 3 4 1 2 3 4

Count: 1 2 3 4 1

Twelve-Bar Boogie

Introducing a new note, low "C" played on the 3rd fret of the "A" or 5th string.

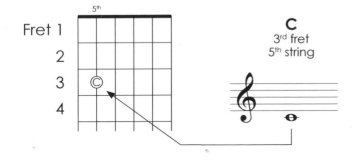

Fret 1

C
3rd fret
5th string

Low "C" is a very important note on the guitar. Study it and practice it very faithfully as you will be using it often in future studies and songs.

Blow the Man Down

Using the new note "C," played with the 3rd finger, 3rd fret on the "A" or 5th string.

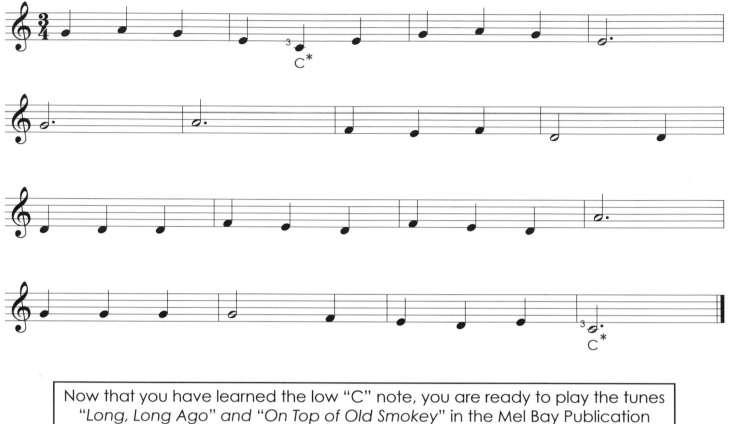

Now that you have learned the low "C" note, you are ready to play the tunes *"Long, Long Ago"* and *"On Top of Old Smokey"* in the Mel Bay Publication *Fun with the Guitar.* Study the melody line.

Schoolhouse Rock
Duet with Chord Accompaniment

Using the new "C" note frequently.

(*) Guitar accompaniment to be played by teacher.

Introducing another new note, low "B" played on the 2nd fret of the "A" or 5th string.

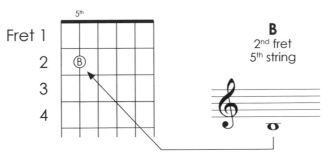

Low "B" and "C" Waltz

Track 38

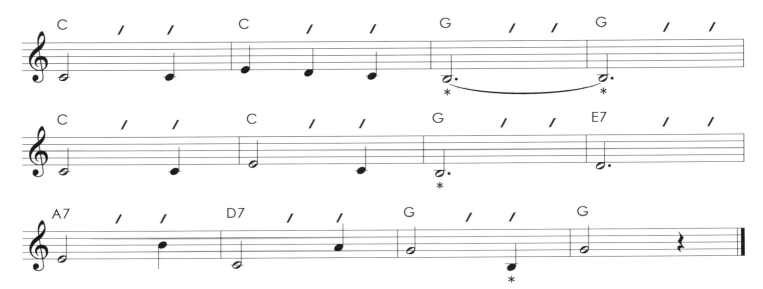

(*) The new "B" note.
(**)Guitar accompaniment to be played by teacher, with discretion, however, the student may play the chords.

Tied Note Study in Three-Quarter Time

Track 39

Using the new notes B and C freely.

(**)Picture charts of all the chords can be found in the Mel Bay Publication *Guitar Chords*.

Introducing the low "A" note which is the open "A" or 5th string.

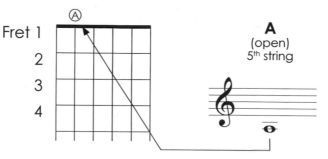

Track 40

Study on the "A" or Fifth String

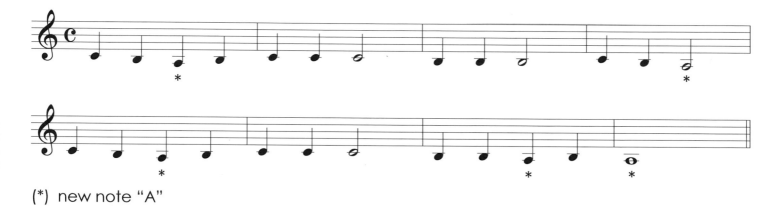

(*) new note "A"

Track 41

My Old Kentucky Home

Stephen Foster

With the exception of the C note in the final measure, the above song is played entirely on the 3rd, 4th and 5th strings.

Review of Notes on the Fifth String (A)

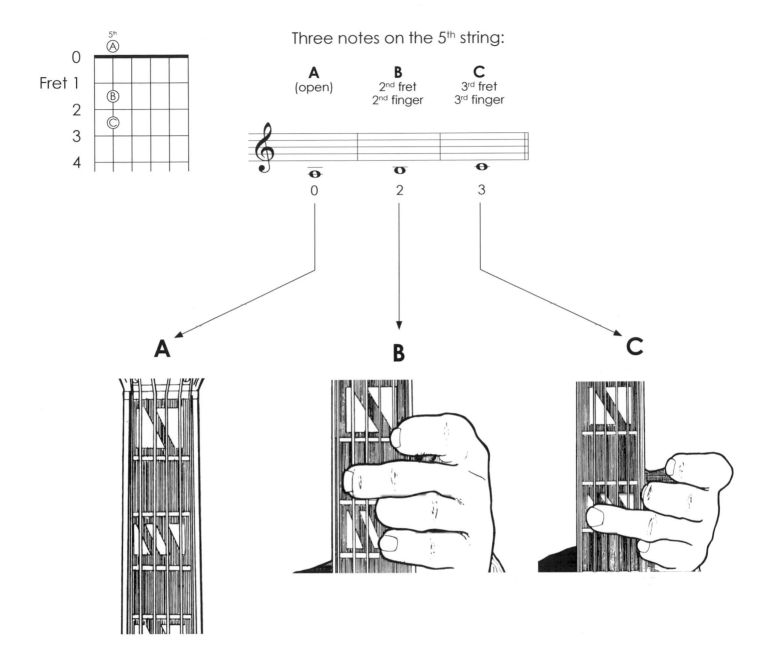

Three notes on the 5th string:

A	B	C
(open)	2nd fret	3rd fret
	2nd finger	3rd finger

Introducing the Sharp (♯)

A sharp sign (♯) placed in front of a note indicates that the pitch of that note is to be raised one fret higher. Each fret represents one-half tone in the scale.

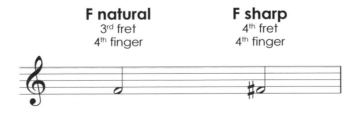

F natural
3rd fret
4th finger

F sharp
4th fret
4th finger

In the following study we will use the F♯ twice, as noted by the * (asterisk).

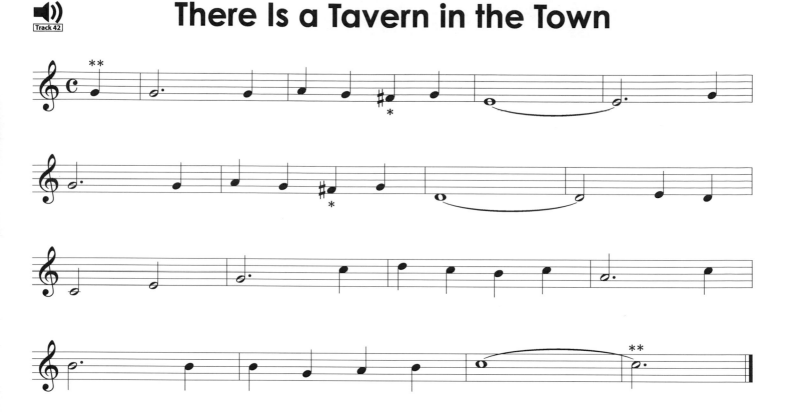

There Is a Tavern in the Town

(*) This is the new note F♯; it is played on the 4th fret of the 4th or D string.

(**) Pick-up note. Observe incomplete measure at end of tune.

> You will find the complete tune *There is a Tavern in the Town*
> in the Mel Bay Publication *Fun with the Guitar*.

Introducing a new note, low "G" played on the 3rd fret of the big "E" or 6th string.

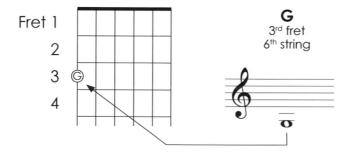

The following tune will use the new note "G" freely.

Good King Wenceslas

(*) The new note "G."

The above song is an excellent study, giving you an opportunity to review the notes on the 4th and 5th strings. Be sure that you know these notes before proceeding.

Faith of our Fathers

More on the use of F#

Introducing two new sharps:

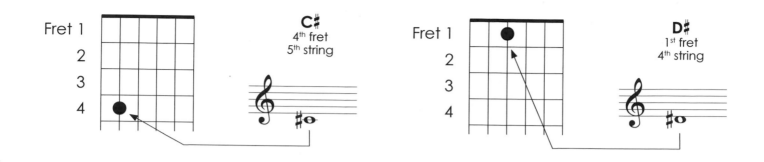

C#
4th fret
5th string

D#
1st fret
4th string

The C# and D# Waltz

(*) All open strings become sharp at the 1st fret.

Introducing low "E," open 6th string and low "F," the 1st fret on the 6th string. These are the last two notes remaining to be learned in the Natural Scale.

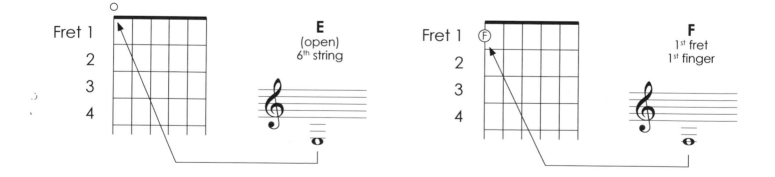

E
(open)
6th string

F
1st fret
1st finger

These two new notes will be used in the following tune.

The Picnic

(*) Low "E," open 6th string
(**) Low "F," 1st fret, 6th string

Introducing the Flat (♭)

A flat (♭) placed in front of a note indicates that the pitch of that particular note is to be lowered one-half tone or one fret lower.

Example

3rd fret   2nd fret   2nd fret   1st fret   2nd fret   1st fret   3rd fret   2nd fret

The circled numbers represent the strings.

The sharp (♯) is **always** played on the same string as the natural, one fret higher. The flat (♭) however, presents a different problem. Although in the above example the flat remains on the same string as the natural, one fret lower, there is one exception, and that is the flat of the **open** string. Obviously, the open string is as low as that note can be played, so then, the flat of the **open** string must of necessity be played on the next *lower* string. It is therefore necessary that you learn the identical note of the open string on the next **lower** string. The chart on the next page will clear up this problem.

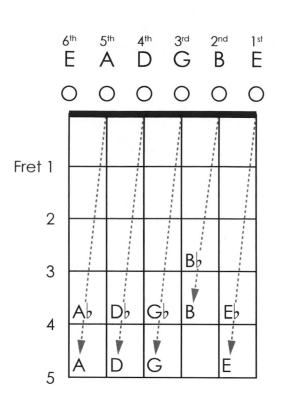

"A" on 5th fret of 6th string is the same as "A" open 5th string.

"D" on 5th fret of 5th string is same as "D" open 4th string.

"G" on 5th fret of 4th string is same as "G" open 3rd string.

"B" on 4th fret of 3rd string is same as "B" open 2nd string.

"E" on 5th fret of 2nd string is same as "E" open 1st string.

The Natural (♮)

A **natural** placed before a note restores that note to its natural or regular position.

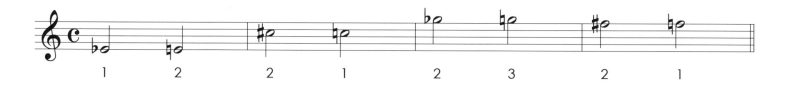

Track 47

A Pair of Naturals

Twelve-Bar Boogie

Making use of the **flat** (♭), the **sharp** (♯), and the **natural** (♮).

(*) B♭, 3ʳᵈ fret, 3ʳᵈ string   (❋) E♭, 4ᵗʰ fret, 2ⁿᵈ string   (❋❋) F♯, 4ᵗʰ fret, 4ᵗʰ string   (❋❋❋) F♮, 3ʳᵈ fret, 4ᵗʰ string

This Old Man Boogie

Using the F Sharp and F Natural signs

(*) F♯, 4ᵗʰ fret, 4ᵗʰ string
(**) F♮, 3ʳᵈ fret, 4ᵗʰ string

The Eighth Note

An **eighth note** receives one-half beat. (One quarter note equals two eighth notes.) It will have a *head*, *stem*, and *flag*. If two or more are in successive order and part of the same beat, they may be connected by a **bar** (see example). The bar is also called a "**beam.**"

Usually, in guitar music, eighth notes with flags will appear when there is only one **eighth** to be played. You will **not** be using these for the present.

Two eighth notes on a beam will be used quite a bit.

Four eighth notes on a beam will be used as often as two on a beam.

The Scale in Eighth Notes

The first part of the scale will be written with two notes on a beam and the rest of it with four notes on a beam.

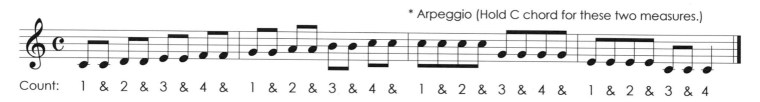

* Arpeggio (Hold C chord for these two measures.)

Count: 1 & 2 & 3 & 4 & 1 & 2 & 3 & 4 & 1 & 2 & 3 & 4 & 1 & 2 & 3 & 4

When beating out the rhythm, the count (1-2-3-4) always occurs when your foot taps **down** and the (&) is when your foot is **up**.

Track 50

Little Brown Jug
Study in Quarter and Eighth Notes

Count: 1　2　3 & 4　1　2　3　4　1 & 2 & 3　4　1　2　3　4

1　2　3 & 4　1　2　3　4　1 & 2　3　4　1　2　3　4

*　The definition of "**arpeggio**" is "*broken chord.*" A more thorough explanation from your teacher will be of great help at this point. Arpeggios will be used a great deal in future studies.

How sharp (♯) and flat (♭) signs affect a particular note within the same measure.

A sharp (♯) or flat (♭) sign placed in front of a note makes *that* note sharp or flat for the rest of the measure, **unless** restored to its regular pitch through the use of the natural (♮) sign. The natural sign (♮) is also known as a **cancellation** sign.

Example:

(*) The ♯ sign in front of the C note makes that note **sharp** throughout the measure.
(**) The ♭ sign in front of the A note makes that note **flat** throughout the measure.

The C♯ and A♭ can only be restored to their natural or regular pitches through the use of a natural (♮) sign.

Example:

Measure no. 1   Measure no. 2

In measure number one, the sharp sign makes the first and second "C's" sharp and the natural sign (♮) cancels the sharp and restores the C notes to their regular pitch.

In measure number two, the flat sign makes the first and second "A's" flat and the natural sign cancels the flat and restores the A notes to their regular pitch.

> For a detailed explanation of the **measure**, review page 5 of this book.

🔊 Study Using Eighth Notes, Sharps and Flats

Track 51

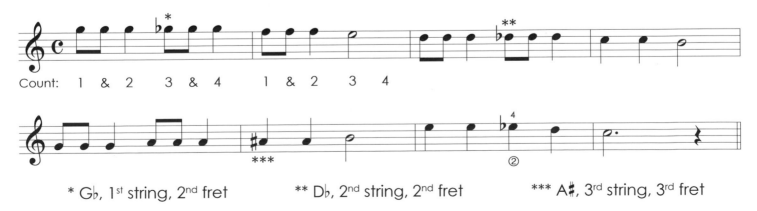

Count: 1   &   2   3   &   4   1   &   2   3   4

* G♭, 1st string, 2nd fret   ** D♭, 2nd string, 2nd fret   *** A♯, 3rd string, 3rd fret

Wildwood Flower

* Observe the incomplete measure, pick-up notes and the incomplete measure at the end.

Eighth-Note Counting Review

Whether two on a beam or four on a beam, they are counted the same.

Count: 1 & 2 & 3 & 4 & 1 & 2 & 3 & 4 &

Square Dance Theme

Track 53

Moderato

Count: 1 2 3 4 1 2 & 3 4

Observe the use of eighth notes throughout. Count steadily and carefully. Also note F♯ in 3rd measure.

> The complete song with lyrics and chord symbols can be found under its original title,
> "*Skip To My Lou*" in the Mel Bay Publication *Fun with the Guitar*.

I've Been Workin' on the Railroad

Track 54

Count: 1 2 3 & 4 &

43

Slow and Easy Blues

Featuring eighth notes and the F#

The guitar accompaniment chords can be found either in the Mel Bay's *Fun with the Guitar* or *Guitar Chords*.

The Scale of C Major in Quarter and Eighth Notes

Scales are very important to the development of technique.

See the Mel Bay Publication *Guitar Technic*.